BROOKLYN BRIDGE

BROOKLYN BRIDGE

LYNN CURLEE

ATHENEUM BOOKS FOR YOUNG READERS

NEW YORK LONDON TORONTO SYDNEY SINGAPORE

Suspended in midair more than 100 feet above New York's East River, the span of Brooklyn Bridge arcs gracefully from shore to shore. The broad roadway linking Brooklyn with Manhattan hangs by a complex web of metal ropes from four gigantic cables, each thicker than a very large man's waist. These cables in turn are slung over the tops of two colossal towers of stone, which are planted firmly in the riverbed and support the entire structure. With the roadway passing through immense pointed arches like those of a cathedral, the towers resemble the monumental gates of an ancient city, while the taut wire ropes have been compared poetically to harp strings.

From the promenade, the bridge's elevated walkway, the spectacular view of Upper New York Bay stretches south, to the Statue of Liberty and beyond. The vast city with its bustling harbor spreads all around. Just to the west, lower Manhattan bristles with skyscrapers, and the energy of America's largest city seems to flow with the traffic through the bridge like an electric current.

When the bridge was built more than a hundred years ago, there were no skyscrapers or automobiles or electricity; most tall buildings were only four or five stories high, and people traveled by horse and carriage. In 1883, when the bridge was completed, its stone towers were the tallest, most massive structures on the continent. Its cables and bridge deck were among the first major constructions anywhere to be made of a metal called "steel," and its span was by far the longest of any bridge in the world.

Its magnificent site, monumental twin towers, breathtaking span, cutting-edge technology, and sheer beauty make Brooklyn Bridge the grandest, and perhaps the most important, structure built in America during the nineteenth century. To people at the time, it seemed almost miraculous. They called it the "Eighth Wonder of the World."

The New York and Brooklyn Bridge, to give its official name, was the masterpiece of an authentic genius, a daring and original engineer whose bridges were works of art. John Augustus Roebling was a German immigrant who had come to America in 1831 at the age of 25. Educated in engineering and philosophy, the brilliant young man began life in America as a farmer and soon started a family. Always ambitious and inventive, Roebling perfected a process for making rope from iron wires. He built a factory for manufacturing his metal rope and in a few years became very wealthy. Then, in early middle age, John Roebling began building bridges.

Although small footbridges hanging from ropes were used in many cultures for centuries, the first real suspension bridge was built in 1796 with a wooden roadway hanging from iron chains. Throughout the first half of the 1800s, many suspended bridges were constructed in both the

John A. Roebling

United States and Europe, but the principles of this new type of construction were not well understood, and several of them collapsed.

Beginning in 1845, John Roebling applied his particular genius to the problem in a series of four large suspension bridges built in the eastern United States. He gradually refined his theories and calculations, constructing longer and longer spans suspended by his iron rope from cables made of wires tightly bound together. Roebling's bridges were stately, stable, and best of all, safe. By the late 1860s, after the American Civil War, he felt he was ready to build the world's biggest bridge.

New York and Brooklyn were two of the nation's largest cities by the mid-nineteenth century. They were independent but separated by less than a half mile of water. Every day thousands of people crossed the treacherous tides of the East River from one city to the other by ferryboat. John Roebling first conceived the great bridge while icebound on one of these ferries in the winter of 1852 with his young son, Washington. In 1867, using the experience he had gained building four similar bridges, Roebling sat down at his drafting table, and in three months the East River bridge was designed and a proposal written. In it Roebling stated: "The completed structure will not only be the greatest bridge in existence, but it will be the greatest engineering work of this continent, and of the age." And so it would be.

NEW YORK
Manhattan Island

NEW
JERSEY

Hudson River

East River

Brooklyn Bridge
in
New York Harbor

Williamsburg Bridge (1903)

Brooklyn
Bridge
(1883)

Manhattan Bridge
(1909)

Ellis Island

Governor's Island

Liberty Island

Brooklyn

Upper New York Bay

N

W   *E*

S

By 1869 legislation was passed authorizing construction of the bridge, and a bridge company of politicians and businessmen from both cities was chartered to finance it. But at the very beginning of the work, tragedy struck. While surveying the river to site the great twin towers, John Roebling was injured in a freak accident. An incoming ferry slammed into the dock where he stood, and his foot, caught between pilings, was crushed. Three weeks later he died a horrible, agonizing death from the rigors of lockjaw. His son, Washington, by now an experienced engineer himself and his father's most valued assistant, was named Chief Engineer of the New York and Brooklyn Bridge. He was 32 years old.

Colonel Washington A. Roebling had served with great distinction during the Civil War, building bridges for the Union army. Modest, quiet, and calm, young Roebling was brave and cool under fire. Like his father, he had a keen mind and an iron will. While serving as a soldier, he met his commanding officer's sister, and they fell deeply in love. Emily Warren was lovely, refined, and very intelligent. The young couple married immediately after the war, and Washington went to work overseeing his father's construction projects.

At the time of his death, John Roebling had worked out the general specifications for his great East River bridge, and when completed, it would look almost exactly like his drawings. But every single detail of the structure had to be individually designed, every stress carefully calculated, and

new techniques invented for its construction on such a vast scale. This was Washington Roebling's task, and it would occupy him and his crew of assistant engineers for the next 14 years.

First of all, each stone tower had to be solidly planted on bedrock underneath many feet of sand, gravel, and mud at the bottom of the river. In the 1870s, without heavy earth-moving equipment, there was no choice but to dig the foundations by hand. To accomplish this, Roebling designed gigantic wooden structures called "pneumatic caissons." Essentially a shallow box, open at the bottom, each caisson was constructed on shore by shipbuilders and launched into the East River. Each was towed to its bridge site like an immense barge and sunk to the riverbed. The caisson was then filled with compressed air generated by steam engines, forcing out the water and providing an airspace in which men could work. As they dug, the stone tower was gradually built up on top, its increasing weight forcing the caisson ever deeper into the riverbed. When bedrock was reached, the airspace inside the caisson would be filled with concrete, solidly grounding the tower.

Although it seemed simple in theory, each caisson was actually a complex structure. Thick sidewalls tapered to a narrow lip covered in iron to act like the edge of a shovel, and the roof was constructed of many layers of solid timbers to support the stonework above. The roof was pierced by shafts of various sizes: small air shafts for lowering supplies, larger water shafts for hauling out the

Cross-Section Through a Caisson

Stone Building Blocks Are Unloaded from Barges

Air Hose

Stone Work

Debris Is Hauled up by Clamshell Scoops and Loaded onto Barges

Air Locks

Supply Shafts

Solid Timber Roof

Shafts for Hauling Debris

Air Space

Blasting

Bedrock

debris, and air locks for the crew to come and go. All was carefully calculated for maintaining the air pressure inside the caisson so that the river would not rush in and drown the workmen.

The Brooklyn caisson was built first and towed into position. It was pumped full of air, and digging began in May 1870. Conditions inside the caisson were appalling. Light was provided by flickering blue-white gas jets and smoking whale oil lamps that cast eerie black shadows. The walls and ceiling were soon covered with slime, and the riverbed floor was a morass of mud and muck. The thick atmosphere was heavy with mist, and the temperature never dropped below 80 degrees. Continually drenched in sweat, most workmen stripped to the waist and wore rubber hip boots to get around. The pressurized air caused "a confused sensation in the head. The pulse was at first accelerated, then sometimes fell below the normal rate. The voice sounded faint and unnatural, and it became a great effort to speak," according to one of Roebling's foremen. He described it as a scene from hell.

Most of the workmen were Irish immigrants. They were grateful for any job, however difficult. But the unpleasant work of digging totally by hand soon proved to be almost impossible. The mud and clay of the riverbed was filled with rocks and huge boulders that had to be broken up before being dug out and hauled away. Roebling had no choice but to try explosives, but no one knew how the pressurized atmosphere would react to a blast. The Chief Engineer courageously conducted experiments alone inside the caisson and determined that small charges carefully placed would work. Inch by laborious inch, the caisson slowly sank into the riverbed while the stonework began rising above the waterline.

Occasionally there were blowouts. As the men dug, the caisson sometimes settled unevenly. This allowed a gigantic bubble of pressurized air to escape from underneath the caisson with explosive speed, jetting from the river like a geyser. Water would pour in to fill the space. It was terrifying to be in the dark caisson during a blowout with the river suddenly rushing in. But the air pressure could be quickly equalized, and blowouts were more frightening than truly life-threatening.

But in December 1870 there was a real disaster. A careless workman left a burning lamp near the ceiling of the caisson, and the wood caught fire. It did not flame or even smoke very much, but smoldering like charcoal embers, the fire was fed and driven by the compressed air deep into the timbers of the caisson roof, where it spread like a cancer. The only way to completely extinguish it was to flood the caisson. After air was pumped back in, it was apparent that large areas of wood would have to be cut away and replaced. Otherwise the rising stonework would come crashing through. The caisson was saved, but the work was set back for months.

Finally, in March 1871, after a year of work, bedrock was reached almost 45 feet below the waterline, the caisson was filled with concrete, and the Brooklyn foundation was complete.

By September the New York caisson was in position, and digging began for the second foundation. In the beginning the work was even more unpleasant than in Brooklyn. For more than a century, this site had been the dumping ground for New York's refuse and raw sewage. Before reaching clean sand and gravel, the crew had to dig through several feet of dense, black, stinking sludge. On this side of the river, there were no boulders, so the work went much faster, and the interior of the New York caisson was lined with iron plates, making it fireproof. But the bedrock here lay far deeper than in Brooklyn—almost 85 feet below the waterline. As the months went by and they dug ever deeper, a new problem arose, insidious and deadly.

At the lower depths, the pressure of the water was so great that the air pressure inside the caisson had to be raised higher and higher to keep out the river. At the end of a work shift, after returning to a normal atmosphere, many workmen experienced excruciating pain in their joints, along with terrible headaches, dizziness, and vomiting. The deeper they dug and the greater the air pressure, the more severe the symptoms became. They called it "caisson disease" or "the bends," since victims usually doubled over in pain. Today we know that after breathing compressed air one must return to a normal air pressure very slowly to prevent gas bubbles from forming in the bloodstream. But in 1872 the cause and cure for the bends were unknown.

On April 22, with the caisson at a depth of 71 feet, a workman died of caisson disease after returning to the surface. Eight days later another man died. The digging was becoming more difficult, since the sand and gravel at this depth was tightly packed like concrete. More and more men were becoming ill, including Roebling. No one went in and out of the pressurized caisson more than the Chief Engineer, and he repeatedly experienced the same suffering as his crew. On May 18 a third man died, and Washington Roebling made the most important decision of his career. He halted the digging at a depth of 78 feet 6 inches, staking the structural integrity of the bridge on his educated opinion that the tower would be stable. Still 6 feet above bedrock, the caisson was filled with concrete, and to this day the New York tower stands solidly on hard-packed sand.

In fact, Roebling himself had almost died. The effects of repeated attacks of the bends ruined his health, almost crippling him, and the agonizing decision to halt the digging apparently caused a nervous breakdown. The Chief Engineer of Brooklyn Bridge was now an invalid, confined to his room and unable to endure the company of anyone except his wife. Although he gradually was able to work as effectively as before, during the eleven years remaining for its construction, Washington Roebling never once returned to the bridge site.

For the next four years, the two towers slowly rose into the sky, eventually dwarfing everything nearby. The granite blocks were brought on barges, then hauled to the top by steam-powered winches and maneuvered into position. At the same time, two huge stone structures were built well inland from each tower. These were the anchorages for securing the ends of the four great cables that would be slung over the tops of the towers. Buried deep within each structure, beneath 60,000 tons of granite, were four gigantic iron anchor plates—one for each cable. The cables would be secured to the anchors by chains of immense iron bars embedded in the stonework and everything held in position by the sheer weight of the granite. Finally, in July 1876, all of the stonework was in place. After seven years, the bridge was half completed.

Cross-Section Through an Anchorage

Cable

Position of the
Roadway on the
Completed Bridge

Iron Chain

Iron Anchor
Buried Under
the Stone Work

On August 14 a 3/4-inch-thick wire rope was unwound across the river from anchorage to anchorage and hoisted to the tops of both towers. Later the same day, another rope was taken across and spliced to the first, forming a continuous loop of wire wrapped at each anchorage around a huge drum. Driven by a steam engine, the endless "traveler" rope was a pulley system for hauling larger cables and supplies across the river. But first, as a symbol that the two cities were now joined, a man made the trip.

The honor went to E. F. Farrington, the bridge's master mechanic. On the morning of August 25, huge crowds gathered on each shore and in boats to view the great event. At about 1:30 P.M., Farrington, dapper in a linen suit and straw hat, seated himself in a sling chair suspended from the traveler rope. As he sailed out over the water, people cheered and boat whistles shrieked. At one point he stood on his precarious seat and saluted the crowds. The entire trip from Brooklyn to New York took 22 minutes.

That autumn the Roeblings returned to Brooklyn from their family home in New Jersey, where the Chief Engineer had gone to recuperate. Though still an invalid, by now he was well enough to return to his own home in Brooklyn Heights, where he could watch the bridge's progress from his bedroom window through powerful field glasses. But he remained a recluse. Already his best friend, nurse, and confidante, Emily Roebling had now become her husband's secretary and

personal assistant. She wrote his letters, helped with working drawings, and served as his eyes and ears, conveying his instructions to the assistant engineers and dealing personally with the trustees and with contractors at the building site. During an era when women were not welcome in the business world, she did all this with great tact and finesse, earning the admiration and respect of everyone involved in the project. Eventually she knew as much as anyone about the techniques of bridge building, and later it was even rumored that she took over as Chief Engineer. While this was untrue, it is certain that without the partnership of his remarkable wife, Washington Roebling could never have completed his task.

By now the bridge was a great public works project. The original Bridge Company was a private organization that raised money by selling stock in the bridge. Several of its members had been totally corrupt, lining their own pockets with money that should have been spent on the bridge. In 1873 the company was dissolved, and a board of trustees was established, with the funds coming directly from the cities of Brooklyn and New York. Brooklyn Bridge would belong to the people.

At the bridge, preparations were made for spinning the four great cables. Using the endless traveler, more wire ropes were hauled across the river and draped over the towers. Five temporary scaffolds called "cradles" were hung from the ropes to give the crew a place to stand while they worked, and a tiny precarious footbridge was built from anchorage to anchorage. Now it was pos-

sible to walk from one city to the other, and the footbridge was actually open to the public for a time. While many of the workmen had been sailors—used to working high up in the rigging of ships—this was a new, exhilarating experience for thousands of men, women, and children who gamely tested their nerve against the great height with only a few planks and wire ropes for support. Occasionally the crew had to rescue someone who was frozen with fear, but no one was injured. The footbridge was closed to the public after the process of cable spinning began in June 1877.

The cables were made of steel wires. Stronger, harder, and more durable than iron, steel was first mass-produced and available in large quantities in the late 1850s. Brooklyn Bridge marks its first use anywhere on such a vast scale. Each wire was about the thickness of a lead pencil, laid parallel, not twisted as in metal rope. Each individual wire was spooled out across the river looped around a "carrier wheel" that was attached to the endless traveler rope. The men in the cradles made sure that every wire hung in the proper curve, exactly parallel to every other wire. When 278 wires had been laid, men rode out in hanging platforms to bind them together every 15 inches with soft wire into a bundle called a "strand." At the anchorages the end of each strand was attached to one of the great iron bars embedded in the stonework, and at the top of the towers the strands for each cable were lowered into an iron "saddle," which held them in position but allowed them to flex and move slightly. Each completed cable was composed of 19 strands and contained 3,515 miles of wire, more than enough to stretch across America from coast to coast.

This intricate process had been invented by John Roebling. It required great precision, and like all phases of the bridge's construction, it involved some danger. Unfortunately, a terrible accident occurred while the cables were being spun. On June 14, 1878, a wire rope holding one of the strands snapped, and the strand lashed about like a gigantic steel whip, killing two men and injuring several others. It was only the most spectacular of several accidents that occurred during the bridge's construction. Including the victims of the bends and John Roebling himself, it is estimated that at least twenty men were killed while working on Brooklyn Bridge.

Only a month after this accident, it was discovered that the manufacturer of the steel cable wire, J. Lloyd Haigh of Brooklyn, was defrauding the bridge by supplying inferior wire for the cables. This was serious business indeed. Roebling's own wire company had not been given the contract because certain board members considered it a conflict of interest, even though Roebling wire was the best available. The Chief Engineer had warned against using Haigh's wire, but the board had voted to do so anyway. The problem could not be fixed because by now the bad wire was spun into the cables along with good wire and could not be removed. Fortunately, the cables had been designed to be six times stronger than necessary. In addition, Haigh was required to supply 150 extra wires for each cable to compensate for the inferior wire. The bridge would be safe.

Cable spinning was completed in October 1878. A tightly coiled spiral of wire was then wrapped around the entire length of each cable, binding it into a solid curving beam of steel. This wire and the steel ropes for suspending the roadway were supplied by the Roebling company.

While the cables were being spun, the bridge approaches were under construction. In both New York and Brooklyn, large areas of each city were bought up and scores of buildings were demolished. In their place a great ramp to support the roadway was built leading up to the top of each anchorage. Architects were hired to fill in the spaces underneath with shops and warehouses, and small bridges were constructed to carry the ramps over cross streets.

Now all was ready for suspending the bridge deck with its roadway. First wrought iron bands were fitted around each cable, and a steel suspender rope was attached to each band. Floor beams made of steel girders were hung from the suspenders. The workmen started at the towers and hung the beams in order toward the anchorages and at the same time toward the center of the bridge. A cagelike trusswork of girders was installed on top of the floor beams to stiffen the entire bridge deck against high winds and vibrations. The trusses also enclosed and defined the roadway, with two outer lanes for carriages, two inner lanes for cable cars, and the elevated promenade for pedestrians in the center. As a finishing touch, steel ropes were strung from the tops of the towers, radiating diagonally to points on the bridge deck, and lashed to the suspender ropes. These diagonal "stays" provided additional stiffening and support and are one of the most beautiful features of the entire structure.

In the midst of this last phase of the construction, Washington Roebling decided to add more steel to further strengthen the bridge deck so that locomotives might be able to cross in the future. This caused some delay and additional expense, and incredibly, several younger members of the

board who had never even met the reclusive Roebling decided that he should be fired after 13 years of brilliant engineering and faithful service. They were voted down by the majority. The man who had built Brooklyn Bridge would finish the job.

Finally, by May 1883, the amazing structure was virtually complete. One beautiful morning, a few days before the official opening, the first horse and carriage was driven across the bridge. As it passed, the remaining workmen removed their hats and gave out a great cheer. Inside there was a single passenger who carried a live rooster in a cage, a traditional symbol of victory. The honor was given to Emily Roebling.

Opening day, May 24, dawned clear and bright. At this early hour, the streets of lower Manhattan and Brooklyn were already thronged with tens of thousands of people, and as the morning wore on, they were joined by tens of thousands more. A grand flotilla of hundreds of ships and pleasure boats jostled for position in the East River. Just before noon, the Atlantic Fleet steamed into New York Harbor, and at about 1:30, after the official party had been driven down Fifth Avenue and Broadway in carriages, the festivities began. Escorted by a regiment of soldiers and a military band, the president of the United States, Chester A. Arthur, along with the governor of New York State and the mayor of New York City, led a delegation of dignitaries on foot across the great bridge. As they passed through the immense arches of the New York tower, they were joined by the bridge trustees. When they reached the Brooklyn tower, they were greeted by more offi-

cials led by the mayor and Emily Roebling. At this moment, the guns of the naval squadron boomed out a salute, and then the entire harbor reverberated with guns, whistles, bells, and cheers. One can only imagine the emotions of Washington Roebling as he watched the celebration alone from his window.

The entire afternoon was given over to speeches and ceremonies as crowds of people walked back and forth on the bridge. In the late afternoon, the official party arrived at the Roebling home in Brooklyn Heights for a reception prepared by Emily. The president, the governor, the two mayors, and all of the other dignitaries came to honor the Chief Engineer for his great achievement and that of his father.

That night the bridge was the scene of a spectacular display of fireworks that lasted a full hour, finishing with a dazzling blaze of five hundred rockets fired at the same moment. At the end of the fireworks, a full moon rose above the two cities, and the electric lights—a brand-new invention that had been installed on the bridge's promenade—were switched on. It was the grandest celebration ever held in America up until that time.

Tragically, only one week later, the bridge was the scene of a terrible disaster. The promenade was crowded with thousands of sightseers when apparently someone yelled out that the bridge was falling. In the general panic, twelve people were crushed to death and scores were injured. On a happier occasion the following year, P. T. Barnum, the master showman, had a lumbering herd of circus elephants driven across the bridge as a publicity stunt. Barnum declared that now he considered the bridge to be safe.

Over the decades, as the means of transportation have changed, so has the bridge. The original cable cars were replaced by trolleys, which in turn were replaced by automobiles, and certain details of the bridge deck were changed to accommodate them. In the 1930s, with the building of gigantic new structures such as San Francisco's Golden Gate Bridge and New York's George Washington Bridge, the East River span lost its title of "World's Greatest Bridge," a status it had held for fifty years. But even the new superbridges owed their success to the design principles perfected by John and Washington Roebling.

Few other works of engineering have ever captured the public imagination in the same way as Brooklyn Bridge. As the nineteenth century neared its end, the bridge was a futuristic vision of the century to come, with its steel span and electric lights. During the twentieth century, the great bridge was celebrated as the subject of poems, paintings, and photographs and as a setting in novels, plays, and movies. And now, at the dawn of the twenty-first century, it is still one of the greatest landmarks and grandest sights of New York, despite the fact that the twin towers that once dwarfed the buildings of the city are now themselves dwarfed by the glittering skyscrapers of Manhattan.

Brooklyn Bridge will go down in history as one of the finest achievements of the American spirit. As one architectural critic wrote: "It so happens that the work which is likely to be our most durable monument, and to convey some knowledge of us to the most remote posterity, is a work of bare utility; not a shrine, not a fortress, not a palace, but a bridge."

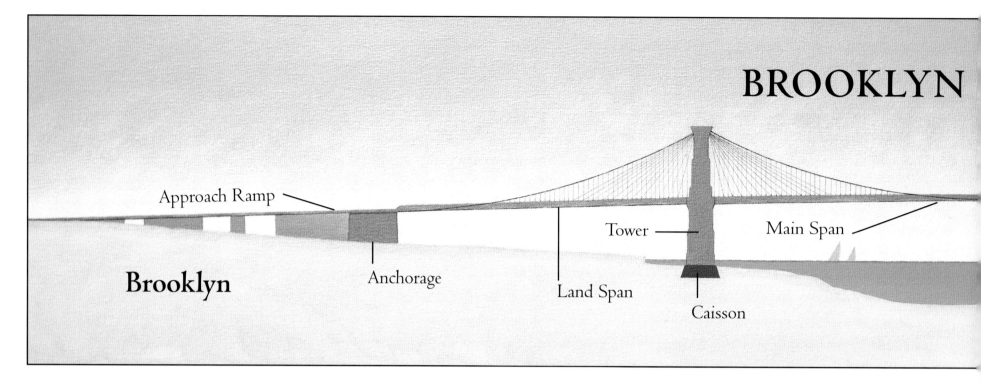

BROOKLYN

Approach Ramp

Tower

Main Span

Brooklyn

Anchorage

Land Span

Caisson

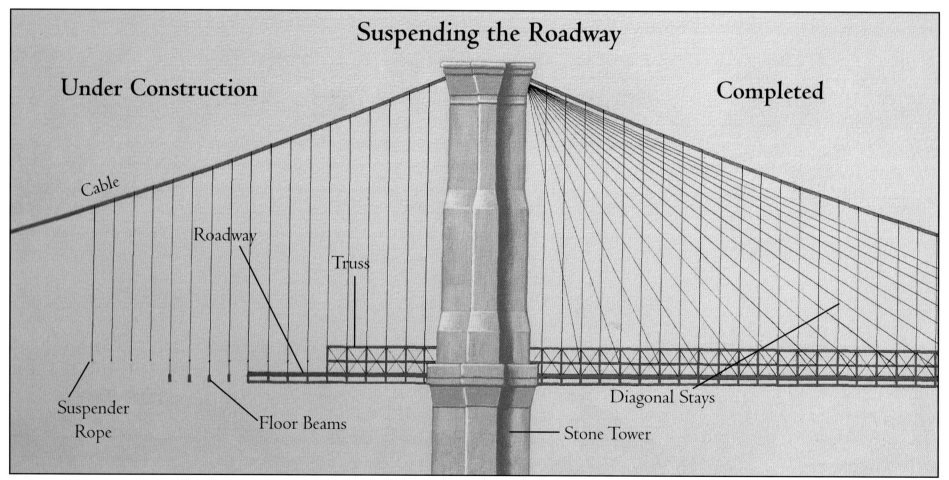

Suspending the Roadway

Under Construction

Completed

Cable

Roadway

Truss

Suspender Rope

Floor Beams

Diagonal Stays

Stone Tower

BRIDGE

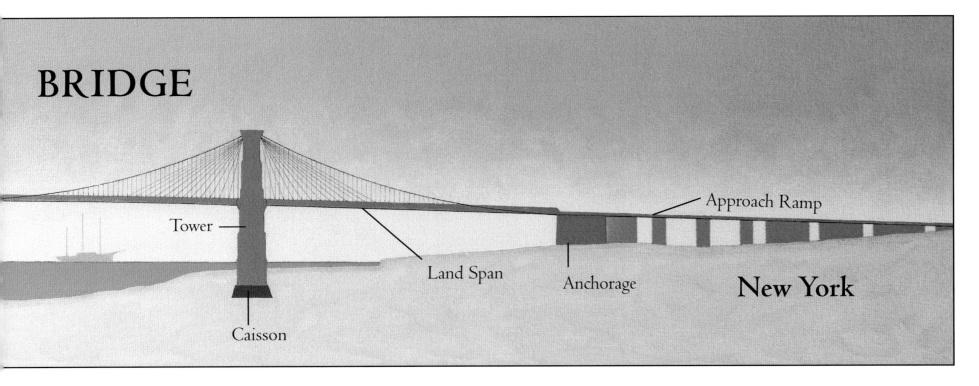

Tower

Caisson

Land Span

Anchorage

Approach Ramp

New York

Cross-Section Through the Bridge Deck

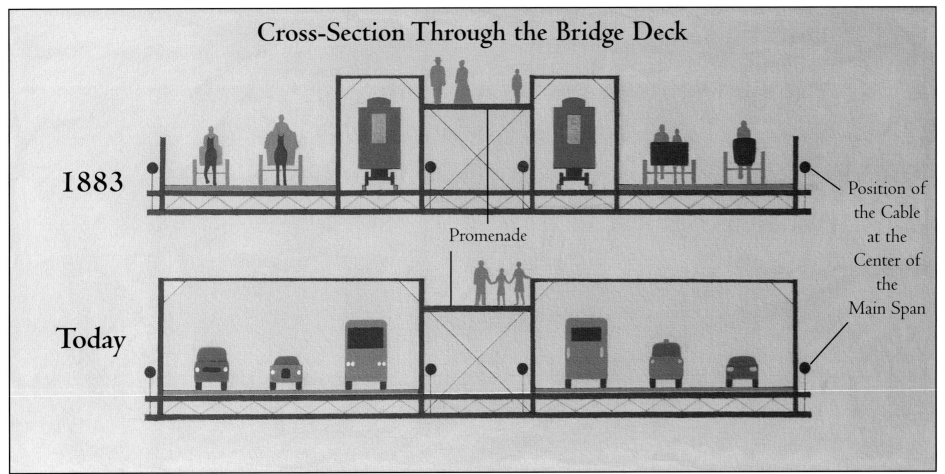

1883

Today

Promenade

Position of
the Cable
at the
Center of
the
Main Span

SPECIFICATIONS

Length of center span: 1,595 feet 6 inches
Length of each land span: 930 feet
Total length of bridge, including approach ramps: 5,989 feet
Width of bridge deck: 85 feet
Height of the central span above waterline: 135 feet
Number of cables: 4
Length of a cable: 3,578 feet 6 inches
Diameter of a cable: 15 3/4 inches
Total length of wire in a cable: 3,515 miles
Weight of a cable: 1,732,086 pounds
Number of suspender ropes hanging from a cable: 380
Depth of Brooklyn foundation: 44 feet 6 inches
Depth of New York foundation: 78 feet 6 inches
Total height of each tower above waterline: 276 feet 6 inches
Height of arches above roadway: 117 feet
Width of each arch: 33 feet 9 inches
Height of the front of each anchorage: 89 feet
Weight of each anchorage: 60,000 tons
Number of anchor plates: 8
Weight of each anchor plate: 23 tons
Total weight of bridge, except for the stonework: 14,680 tons

TIMELINE

1867 - John Roebling begins designing the bridge

1869 - First surveys to position the bridge

July 22: John Roebling dies

1870 - Brooklyn caisson is launched and towed into position

Digging begins and stonework is started

December 1: Fire in the caisson

1871 - March 11: Brooklyn foundation is completed

New York caisson is launched and towed into position

Digging begins and stonework started

1872 - May 18: Washington Roebling decides to stop the

descent of the caisson

July 12: New York foundation is completed

1873 - Work begins on the anchorage structures

1874 - Work continues on towers and anchorages

1875 - June: Brooklyn tower is completed

1876 - July: New York tower is completed and anchorages are finished

August 14: The endless traveler rope is stretched across the river

August 25: E. F. Farrington crosses the river

1877 - June: Cable spinning begins

1878 - July: Wire fraud discovered

October: Cable spinning is completed

1881 - Floor beams are suspended from the cables

1883 - April: Trusswork, roadway, and promenade are completed

May 24: Brooklyn Bridge is opened

For Douglas

BIBLIOGRAPHY

Brooklyn Museum. *The Great East River Bridge, 1883-1983.* New York: Harry N. Abrams, 1983.

Jacobs, David, and Anthony E. Neville. *Bridges, Canals, and Tunnels.* New York: American Heritage, 1968.

McCullough, David. *The Great Bridge.* New York: Simon & Schuster, 1972.

Schodek, Daniel L. *Landmarks in American Civil Engineering.* Cambridge, Massachusetts: M.I.T. Press, 1987.

Atheneum Books for Young Readers

An imprint of Simon & Schuster Children's Publishing Division

1230 Avenue of the Americas

New York, New York 10020

Copyright © 2001 by Lynn Curlee

Book design by Ann Bobco and Jim Hoover

The text of this book is set in Deepdene H.

The illustrations are acrylic paintings reproduced in full color from photographic transparencies.

Mr. Curlee would like to thank Ed Peterson for photographing the paintings.

Printed in Hong Kong

2 4 6 8 10 9 7 5 3 1

Curlee, Lynn.

Brooklyn Bridge / written and illustrated by Lynn Curlee.—1st ed.

p.   cm.

Includes bibliographical references.

Summary: Describes the planning, construction, and history of the Brooklyn Bridge,

celebrated as one of the greatest landmarks and grandest sights of New York City.

ISBN 0-689-83183-8

1. Brooklyn Bridge (New York, N.Y.)—Juvenile literature. 2. Bridges—New York—Design and construction—Juvenile literature. [1. Brooklyn Bridge (New York, N.Y.) 2. Bridges—

Design and construction.] I. Title.

TG25.N53.C87 2001

624'.5'097471—dc21   99-43771

FIRST EDITION